Original title:
Existential Adventures in the Supermarket

Copyright © 2025 Creative Arts Management OÜ
All rights reserved.

Author: Juliana Wentworth
ISBN HARDBACK: 978-1-80566-052-1
ISBN PAPERBACK: 978-1-80566-347-8

Forks and Futures

In the aisle of dreams, I start to roam,
My cart's a ship, my list, a tome.
A fork debates the fate of spaghetti,
While lettuce winks, feeling quite petty.

The ketchup bottle wobbles with glee,
Tomatoes whisper, 'Pick me, can't you see?'
A box of cereal grins with a crunch,
"Join me at breakfast," it says with a munch.

The Poetry of Price Tags

Price tags sing their witty little song,
They dance with decimals, join the throng.
A coupon whispers sweet nothings in my ear,
"Save a penny, oh dear, hold me near!"

A clearance rack calls, "I'm a bargain divine!"
As I fill my cart with deals that align.
Summer fruits flash like a poet's bold line,
While frozen dinners rehearse for prime time.

Walks Among the Wares

I stroll between aisles, a curious sight,
Where chips plot to crunch in the dead of night.
Soap suds serenade me with frothy delight,
While spices trade stories, oh what a fright!

Canned beans debate who's the best of the can,
In a hierarchy only the peas can understand.
A baguette rolls by, cheeky and spry,
"Who needs a recipe? Just let it fly!"

Discerning the Divine in Dietary Choices

A kale leaf preaches health with great flair,
While donuts promise joy, without a care.
Chocolate chips conspire in the grain aisle,
"Let's tempt fate," they say, "with a smile!"

Eggs argue yolk vs. white in their tray,
"Don't break us apart, it just ruins the play."
I laugh at the antics, marvel at fate,
As I ponder my choices while veggies await.

Musing Among the Milk

Amidst the cartons stacked so high,
I ponder if cows ever sigh.
Should I pick almond or the oat?
Will my smoothie float or simply gloat?

Creamy dreams in a fridge so cold,
Do dairy delights have stories untold?
I laugh at my choices, so vast and absurd,
Finding joy in labels, each one a word.

The Grocery List of Life.

A list of hopes scribbled on a page,
Bananas of wisdom, and bread of sage.
Each item a wish, a flavor we crave,
But will I remember, or simply misbehave?

Eggs for the mornings, so bright and round,
Yet most days I scramble without making sound.
Tomatoes for passion, but passion's a mess,
What if my salad holds more than excess?

The Aisles of Infinite Choices

Rows of potential stretch far and wide,
Each shelf a journey, each can a guide.
Chips made with laughter, or salsa with spice,
Decisions unravel—oh, how they entice!

Should I take a risk on exotic cheese?
Or stick with my favorite, it's sure to please.
The colorful labels all shout and they sing,
In this quirky bazaar of everything!

Cart Full of Questions

In my cart, I gather hopes and dreams,
Spaghetti of fate and chocolate of schemes.
Why does this aisle feel like a maze?
Numbers and letters in a grocery haze?

I reach for a snack, then ponder its worth,
Is happiness found in a bag or the earth?
A mystery unwrapped with every new bite,
Life's flavors swirl in the fluorescent light.

Price Tags as Philosophers

On shelves they whisper, truths in price,
A dollar here, a dime is nice.
In clearance racks, we ponder fate,
Is savings luck, or just more weight?

They argue fate in neon signs,
"Buy one, get one," a world that shines.
Discounts beckon, choices loom,
Why is bread a metaphor for doom?

The Pulse of Pavement underfoot

Each step on tiles, a rhythmic beat,
Squeaky carts and shoelaces meet.
Just past the fruit, life's mirth unfolds,
As apples whisper secrets bold.

Lettuce shuffles, calls for cool,
Tomatoes blush in this strange school.
Each aisle's a journey, paths depart,
The checkout line, a work of art.

Searching for Meaning in Frozen Meals

In icy shelves, deep thoughts reside,
Potatoes wave, they took a ride.
How can a burger have a soul?
A cheese-trapped life, the frozen goal.

Dinners beckon, quick and bland,
Are they a way to understand?
Noodles swirl in a postmodern fate,
As hungry voices loudly debate.

The Echoes of Aisle Conversations

Whispers wander through bread and cheese,
"Do we need this?" "Just buy with ease!"
In the cereal aisle, life's a jest,
Frosted flakes or wisdom's quest?

Cart wheels spin with laughter's glee,
Lost in thoughts, who will we be?
Among the snacks, aspirations rise,
Shredded dreams beneath glittering skies.

Lost in the Grocery's Labyrinth

Wandered past the yogurt aisle,
Thought I'd found a secret file.
Between the cheese and clammy meat,
I lost my way, can't feel my feet.

A cart with wheels that squeak and whine,
Drifting down the snack food line.
Caught in a maze of boxes and bags,
Each corner turned, my mind unflags.

The cereal towers loom and rise,
Like monuments to our food lies.
I chase the whims of hunger's call,
In this grocery store, I've lost it all.

Yet still I search for coupon gold,
In each aisle a new world unfolds.
With laughter echoing aisle to aisle,
I find my way, if just for a while.

The Lost Art of Picking Produce

Tomatoes blushing, apples bright,
Pick the best one, what a fright!
Is this fruit ripe or just a joke?
Or is it hiding some leafy cloak?

I shake the melons, feel the weight,
Does that mean freshness, or just fate?
Avocados, are they firm or soft?
Questions swirl, like a chef's old scoff.

Broccoli trees with crowns so proud,
But do people really eat them loud?
I juggle oranges, try to devise,
A strategy, but look, here come spies!

Is this the melon of my dreams?
Or shall I leave with only schemes?
In the end, I just grab a pack,
Of frozen peas—it's time to snack!

A Symphony of Senses

The scent of bread, warm and sweet,
Dances with cheese, a perfect treat.
The melons sing a ballad bright,
In colors that can dazzle sight.

Crackling chips play a crunchy beat,
While frozen peas just tap their feet.
A symphony of tastes and more,
Each aisle beckons to explore.

Cart wheels squeaking like a band,
As apples roll, they take a stand.
Ketchup bottles sing a tune,
While candy bars play like a cartoon.

With every step a note is played,
In this market concert, fears fade.
So grab your cart and join the fun,
In this grocery orchestra, we're all one.

The Checkout Line of Life Decisions

In the checkout line, I ponder deep,
Should I buy the chips or get some sleep?
The candy bars glare with sugar's might,
While pasta whispers, 'Make tonight bright.'

The magazines flaunt a life of glam,
While I just want a good old ham.
Do I need a snack for this long ride?
Or should I splurge on ice cream and pride?

The cashier awaits with her knowing smile,
While my choices taunt me every mile.
Do I go healthy, or treat myself right?
Each item feels like a cosmic fight.

At last, I reach out for my prize,
A last-minute chocolate, oh how it lies!
With a wink, I pay and leave the store,
Such profound decisions; who could ask for more?

The Strangeness of Everyday Choices

In the land of cereal boxes,
I ponder over flakes and puffs,
With marshmallows or nuts my main blockers,
Decisions feel quite tough.

Which aisle holds all my dreams?
Is it snacks or frozen peas?
A dance with indecision, it seems,
As I dodge the late-night keys.

Do I go for chips or dip?
Or just a simple soda pop?
The list is long, I lose my grip,
On choices that just won't stop.

What price for a can of beans?
Is it worth a second glance?
Or is this where all life convenes?
In the checkout line, we prance.

The Philosophy of Discounts

Why is there wisdom in a sale?
Buy one, get one free, a tale,
As I wrestle with coupon fate,
Do discounts create or deflate?

The price tag laughs, it's quite absurd,
A game of math, I feel like a nerd,
Yet taking two feels like a score,
What if I get just one more?

In this carnival of price and worth,
Is a discount a blessing or curse?
I save a dime, but what do I gain?
Another bottle of ketchup, insane!

Suddenly, a chef's hat appears,
I cook gourmet with flair and cheers,
Yet in truth, it's chopped-up fries,
Now which aisle holds my pie in disguise?

Between Berries and Bananas

Strawberries wink, while bananas grumble,
In this shady produce scramble,
Do I mix them for a smoothie delight,
Or leave them alone, out of sight?

The cosmic dance of fruits begins,
Berries whisper, where it spins,
Should I risk the ripe for the right?
What's in the cart feels ever tight.

Tangled in choices, I stand aghast,
Bananas chuckle, "You're outclassed!"
But I grab both, it feels quite fine,
A fruity feast, a balance divine.

And so I strut, proud of my haul,
With laughter echoing down the hall,
In the land of snacks, I know it's true,
Life's a blend of red and yellow too.

The Metaphor of the Grocery Basket

My basket rolls, a world in tow,
Each item holds a tale to show,
A loaf of bread, a pair of socks,
Deep questions dwell in my food stocks.

The milk is truth, both fresh and white,
Eggs are dreams that take to flight,
While chocolate bars whisper sweet lies,
Do I really need these daily spies?

Cereal represents the morning grind,
Coffee speaks of the battles in mind,
And frozen peas are the friends I keep,
Life's little joys, mildly cheap.

As I check out, I ponder fate,
What fills my basket does not equate,
To fullness found in simple cheer,
It's the journey that brings us here.

Aisles of Abstraction

In the cereal aisle, I met a ghost,
He claimed to be the toast of breakfast's coast.
With Lucky Charms, he danced and twirled,
While I wondered if sanity ever swirled.

Next came the pasta, with a saucy grin,
Spaghetti strands won't let the laughter thin.
They whispered secrets, of carbon and heat,
As I balanced my choices, oh, what a feat!

The Cart's Confession

My shopping cart speaks, it's quite the chatty thing,
Claiming it's tired of carrying all my bling.
"More avocados?" it groans with a sigh,
"Next time, let's just roll through the candy aisle, why?"

It dreams of a life without fruits and greens,
Just Skittles and chocolate, oh, what fun scenes!
We'd zoom down the lanes, a joyride spree,
But alas, here we are, amidst broccoli!

Wandering Between Produce and Philosophy

In the vegetable section, I pondered a bit,
Do carrots dream of being salad, or just sit?
The lettuce looked wise, with its leaves all entwined,
Offering wisdom that made my thoughts grind.

A potato chimed in, with a starchy reply,
"Life's all mashed up, my friend, give it a try!"
The fruits chimed along, each one with a tale,
I laughed at their stories, as I searched for a pale.

Shelves of Solitude

In the quiet aisle, I found my own space,
Among the zany snacks, I took my place.
The chips were all gossiping, oh what a scene,
While cookies conspired, like a sugary dream.

Fizzy drinks bubbled with laughter and cheer,
While frozen dinners whispered, "We're always near."
I joyfully strolled, my heart feeling light,
In this pantry of whimsy, everything felt right.

Between the Sorrows of Snacks

In the aisle of crispy chips,
A dance of flavors, my tastebuds flip.
Popcorn's waltz, pretzels sway,
Junk food sings, come join the play.

Candy bars in a bright parade,
Sweets and treats, a luscious trade.
Nutrition's whisper lost in fun,
Chocolate dreams, why not? Just one!

Beneath the shelves, my choices swell,
Do I buy snacks or just rebel?
Raisins mock, while cookies grin,
In this snack jungle, where to begin?

Trolley rolls like a laughter spree,
Each item shouts, "Come snack with me!"
Between the sorrows, joy's in stock,
With every munch, I hear it talk.

Unpacking the Carnality of Consumption

In carts of bounty, cravings peek,
Savory whispers, cheek to cheek.
Bagels blush, croissants tease,
In this market, I find my ease.

Sauces drip with pure desire,
Flavors clash, a taste bud choir.
Every label, a siren's call,
Will I indulge? I just might fall.

Pasta twirls in a sultry dance,
A creamy dream, it takes a chance.
Eggplants wink from the side display,
This love affair leads me astray!

From shelf to shelf, my heart does race,
Each item chosen, a daring embrace.
In this ritual, I find delight,
Consuming life, all day, all night.

The Teetering Pile of Choices

A mountain forms of canned delights,
Stacked like dreams on sleepless nights.
One more item, just one last chip,
Balancing snacks on a shopping trip.

Tomato sauce in bright, bold jars,
Pasta shapes like distant stars.
Will I conquer this towering feat,
Or end up with a pile of cheat?

Frozen meals in a chilly row,
Riding the wave of a meal-time flow.
Do I choose Italian or spicy Thai?
The teetering tower makes me sigh.

As I ponder with a furrowed brow,
To each selection, I take a vow.
Amidst the chaos, I laugh so loud,
In choices vast, I feel so proud.

Almost Lost in the Dairy Dream

In the fridge's glow, yogurt's bright,
A tasty promise in the late night.
Cheeses whisper from the back,
"Come here, dear friend, join our snack!"

Milk cartons line up, a dairy crew,
With cream and butter, what should I do?
Ice cream tubs in a frosty dance,
In this realm, I'll take my chance.

Slipping past with a buttered grin,
Oh, how my heart does leap and spin.
Almost lost in this creamy stream,
Dairy dreams do weave and gleam.

A scoop of joy, a slice of glee,
In the land of dairy, I'm wild and free.
With every bite, I taste the thrill,
Almost lost, but never still.

Stolen Moments in the Snack Lane

In the aisle where chips collide,
I munch away with dreams inside.
Should I choose cheese or spicy heat?
Life's big questions at my feet.

A cart rolls by with cosmic grace,
Is that the cashier or my fate's embrace?
Soda pop and candy bars,
A galaxy of sugar stars.

Caught in a pickle, I browse the spread,
Life's deep thoughts on sour bread.
Frozen pizza whispers 'stay,'
As I simply lose my way.

In snack lanes, joy feels renowned,
Finding truths where joy is found.
With each bite, I trip and cheer,
Snack time wisdom—deliciously clear.

Shopping for Answers

Toilet paper rolls, a grand debate,
Do I need two or just one fate?
The price tag laughs, a quirky riddle,
Choosing brands feels like a fiddle.

In the fruit section, I ponder deep,
Why do apples in pairs always leap?
Bananas grin, all yellow and bright,
As I question my life's delight.

Checking out snacks, a bag in each hand,
Am I a philosopher, or just bland?
The checkout line—a queue to reflect,
On the choices, I sometimes neglect.

Each item scanned holds tales untold,
Of joys and quirks, both timid and bold.
I pay with laughter, life's currency bright,
Shopping for answers, with each silly bite.

An Odyssey of the Ordinary

Trolley wheels squeak with tales of lore,
In this oversized jungle, I roam the floor.
Am I a hero with milk on my quest?
Or just a wanderer seeking the best?

The cereal boxes talk in delight,
Each character winks, oh what a sight!
In the land of frosted flakes and cheer,
I gather courage, dispelling fear.

Bottled water stares, calm like a sage,
While pasta shapes dance in a page.
Can a sauce really change my view?
In this epic tale, it's all about you.

I stumble upon juice, spilling the truth,
A splash of color from the fountain of youth.
In this ordinary circus, I find my groove,
An odyssey beckons, enjoy the move!

Reality Between Racks

Amidst the shelves, life feels surreal,
With each aisle, I spin the wheel.
Do I take snacks or craft my health?
In this conundrum lies my wealth.

Hiding behind that giant box,
A philosopher debates with dirty socks.
The broccoli shouts, 'Make the right choice!'
While donuts politely raise their voice.

Cart wheels humming, a quirky tune,
Shopping cart dreams by the light of the moon.
Gummy bears giggle in candyland,
While I grasp fate with a steady hand.

Reality fights with chips in a pack,
With every bite, I'm never off track.
Between the racks, laughter collides,
Shopping for dreams where humor resides.

The Philosophy of the Last Can

In the aisle of canned delights,
A lone can winks in the night.
Is it fate or just a prank?
I ponder while I hold it dank.

The labels laugh, they talk in rhyme,
Should I take it? Or is it crime?
On the shelf it sits, all forlorn,
I reach for it, a bond is born.

But what's inside? A mystery true,
Perhaps it's soup, or a stew for two.
I weigh my choices, heart in hand,
Oh, deep thoughts in this canned land!

Last can standing, it knows my fears,
We share the weight of all these years.
Together we roll to the checkout line,
Philosophy bought, for just a dime!

Unraveling Reality Among the Eggs

Among rows of shells, so pristine,
I wonder, what's truly seen?
These oval orbs hold secrets vast,
Do they tell tales of the future, past?

In each carton, a life-held plan,
Who knew eggs had such a span?
Are they drifters, or destined clowns?
While I juggle thoughts, they wear crowns.

I crack one open, a yolk so bright,
It leads me to ponder, day and night.
Do they hope for omelets, or just to roam?
In this market, I create my home.

Gathered here, they quietly cluck,
A symphony in this place of luck.
With each purchase, I join the show,
Adventures laid out in a row!

Choices in Cart

In a cart that's far from empty,
Lies a battle, oh so plenty.
Do I take the chips or the fruit?
Each item screams, "I'm so cute!"

Bread calls softly, "I'll make you toast,"
While cupcakes whisper, "You'll love me most."
A dance of cravings, wild and free,
Which will shine? Which will flee?

The salad rolls its eyes at junk,
While candy seduces with a funk.
Choices abound, a feast of fun,
Yet my cart feels like a loaded gun.

With every turn through the endless rows,
I dodge disaster, as chaos grows.
Finally, I check out—a merry mix!
Life's odd tapestry, in grocery fix!

Aisle Twelve: Echoes of Introspection

Aisle twelve, where thoughts collide,
I wander lost, nowhere to hide.
Beverages dance, they shimmer and sway,
I sip my doubts, drowning in play.

Each label like a puzzled face,
Do they ponder their time in this place?
Juices whisper tales of cheer,
While sodas giggle, echoing near.

I stumble past the snacks and treats,
Contemplating life's quirks and beats.
A row of chips turns to me and grins,
"Join the fun where chaos begins!"

So I chuckle loud, make my own fun,
In this nutty store, my journey spun.
As I leave with whims and laughter great,
Aisle twelve has shaped my fate!

Echoes of Price Tags Forgotten

In aisles where memories fade away,
Loyal shoppers lose their way.
Discount signs wave like a flag,
Would a frozen pizza dare to brag?

Carts collide like bumper cars,
Chasing cereal dreams beneath the stars.
A mystery in every shelf they find,
Are those peas really left behind?

Clipping coupons for a dollar store thrill,
Is it worth it? Only time will tell.
Amidst the chaos and grocery scheme,
Life's but a chance, or so it seems!

So laugh with me in this food bazaar,
Where prices sometimes feel bizarre.
Between the snacks and meal preps galore,
What is real? Oh, who keeps score?

The Produce Section's Philosophical Produce

In a basket of dreams where tomatoes lay,
Do carrots ponder what they'll say?
Apples debate what's ripe or not,
While broccoli's plans go up in a knot.

A cucumber whispers, 'Am I too cool?'
As peppers argue who's the best in school.
Lettuce giggles at the myths it hears,
Mint's fresh thoughts leave others in tears.

The avocados claim they're the toast of the town,
While split peas watch with a frown.
In this leafy forum, the wisdom abounds,
Yet who organizes the salads around?

Oh, shelves of insight, a leafy affair,
Vegetables gossip without a care.
Produce philosophers in a row,
Perhaps we should linger, and let these thoughts grow.

Savoring Moments in Canned Reflections

Splendid rows of soups, a symphony bright,
Can we compare to the stars in the night?
Beans come and go, like friends in a bind,
What stories they'll share, if only we find.

The labels boast tales of flavor and fun,
Yet mystery lurks under every can run.
Peaches in syrup dream of the sun,
While sardines sparkle — they've barely begun!

Pop the lid open, hear moments resound,
The laughter of beans is quite profound.
In the reflections of glass, time stands still,
Is a can just a meal, or a testament of will?

Time in the pantry can teach us a lot,
Partake in the tales, give the past a shot.
For even in cans, life has its glee,
A picnic of flavors, just waiting for thee!

The Lemon's Zest of Life's Dilemmas

A lemon sits high on a shelf of delight,
Twirling and pondering what's wrong and right.
Should I be lemonade or a fancy tart?
Echoes of zest flare, deep in the heart.

Life's a squeeze, said the lime with a grin,
Are we bitter or sweet? Where do we begin?
Fruit salads debate on a plate of regrets,
As the oranges laugh while they make their bets.

The zest of existence, a hit or a miss,
Can citrus provide the ultimate bliss?
Amidst all the juicing and balancing acts,
Life's conundrums are bittersweet facts.

So peel off your worries, let juice flow free,
With a twist of the rind, we can just be.
In this quirky market maze, take a chance,
For life's fruity puzzles may lead to romance!

Filling the Cart

In the cart, a mix of dreams,
Potato chips and ice cream themes.
A cereal jungle, so absurd,
Lost my list, now it's all a blur.

Checkout lines, a testing fate,
Grocery clerks who seem to wait.
The pulse of life in canned peas sings,
While I ponder what tomorrow brings.

Emptiness in the Soul

Staring blankly at the shelf,
Reflecting like a ghost myself.
Oranges rolled, a citrus tease,
Feeling light, like autumn leaves.

The salad greens are crisp and bright,
But dare I dive into this bite?
A trip for snacks turns into strife,
As I question the meaning of life.

Aisle Four and the Weight of Existence

Aisle four, where the chaos reigns,
Lost in thought, slashing at chains.
Butter and bread, what a paradox,
Weighed down by my thoughts, like a box.

I grab a loaf, then put it back,
What's the point of this whole snack attack?
Rummaging through jars of fate,
As time slips by, I contemplate.

Grappling with Bananas and Mortality

Bananas piled in a bright display,
"But will they ripen?" I start to sway.
In a world where the fruit can fade,
Am I just a joke that life has made?

With each peel, a layer of truth,
Caverns of thought fuel the heart of youth.
Munching on yellow, I start to laugh,
While musing on the cosmic path.

Coupons and Cosmic Questions

Waving coupons, feeling grand,
While pondering the infinite plan.
Do discounts hold the truth we seek?
Or just a cheap way to feel unique?

The frozen foods whisper their plight,
As I grasp for reason, through the night.
With every clip and every save,
I laugh at how the madness gave.

The Half-Empty Cart as a Life Metaphor

My cart's a little light, what does that mean?
A balance of wonders, and just a few greens.
Do I go for the chips, or the fancy cheese?
Decisions like these always bring me to my knees.

With every item placed, a choice that feels grand,
Am I shopping for joy or just things I can't stand?
The checkout line whispers, 'What's worth the weigh?'
In this half-empty world, I'll just roll with the play.

In the Realm of Salad Dressings

Bottles line the shelves, a rainbow so bright,
Each one sings a story, quite the tasty sight.
Ranch calls me gently, while balsamic barks loud,
A dressing for every mood, I'd make quite a crowd.

Do I go with the creamy, or stick with the spice?
Each bottle's a door to a flavorful slice.
Will I drown my greens or give them a wink?
In this dressing dilemma, I ponder and think.

The Existential Produce Picker

In the land of fresh fruits, I wander and roam,
Picking apples and berries, feeling right at home.
Is this peach too soft, or the kiwi too weird?
Shopping for wisdom, I'm slightly bemused and jeered.

Carrots stand tall with a crunchy allure,
While broccoli whispers, 'I'm healthy, for sure!'
What defines my choices, these vegetables bold?
Are they nourishing dreams or just stories untold?

Life Lessons in Aisle Seven

In Aisle Seven's glow, the cereal boxes cheer,
Sugary promises dance, 'Come taste your childhood here!'

Do I go for the flakes or the marshmallow shapes?
Each box holds a memory, wrapped up in escapes.

Beneath the bright logos, wisdom is hidden,
The choice of my breakfast feels oh-so forbidden.
Do I reach for the fun or the health on the side?
In this hollow aisle, my thoughts collide and hide.

In Search of the Perfect Tomato

In the aisle of reds, I roam,
Searching the perfect fruit to call home.
Round and plump, with a glossy sheen,
Is this the one I've always dreamed?

The checkout line mocks my quest,
As I wonder if this one's the best.
With every poke, the ripeness fades,
Yet coupons on these flaws cascades.

My basket's getting heavy now,
But oh dear, I've lost my vow.
A tomato's worth is judged by fate,
Yet here I am, still filling plates.

Beyond Coupons: A Quest for Meaning

With a pocket full of discounts in hand,
I set out to conquer this grocery land.
As I wander through aisle and shelf,
I stumble upon the inner self.

Do I need five boxed cookies? Why not?
Or a three-pack of sauce in a hot pot?
Am I living for deals or for something real?
In this installment, I start to feel.

The mustard's singing a jazzy refrain,
While chips tell tales of a salty plain.
As I scan the register's final fling,
I'm left wondering, what does this new day bring?

Ode to the Out-of-Stock

Ode to the gaps on the grocery shelves,
Where dreams of dinners implode themselves.
No apples, no bread, just a sad empty spot,
Oh, where can I find the snack I forgot?

The aisle of wishes, the land of despair,
One box of cereal left hanging in air.
The search for a muffin, a fierce rollercoaster,
What happened to choices? I'm needing a toaster!

In chaos and clutter, I find some delight,
In the battle of wits, I'll continue the fight.
As items shrink down, my will turns to stone,
Can I grab something fresh before I'm alone?

Life as a Shopping Cart

Life's a cart with wheels that squeak,
Rolling through chaos and sometimes bleak.
Each item tossed in, a choice to be made,
Balancing bread and a new ice cream shade.

Dodging the corners, I bump some poor chap,
"Excuse me," I say, "I'll just take a nap."
Impatient kids whine for just one more snack,
As I navigate through this fun little track.

With coupons in hand and a laugh in my heart,
I ponder if shopping's my true worldly art.
In this ridiculous maze of delight and dismay,
I'll always find joy in the cart's crazy ballet.

Counting Choices

Rows of cereal, a dazzling sight,
Too many flavors, I could lose the fight.
Do I want chocolate? Or perhaps some fruit?
My stomach grumbles, oh what a hoot!

Cart's getting heavy, and so is my mind,
Endless options, what treasures to find?
Pickles or olives, should I go wild?
I think I'll ask my inner child.

Staring at veggies, what do they cost?
Broccoli's green, but am I the boss?
So many choices, it's making me dizzy,
Should I go healthy, or get something fizzy?

Finally at checkout, just loading the loot,
But wait, they charge for the plastic bag, shoot!
One last decision, I'm running out of time,
Should I splurge for the candy, or stick to the rhyme?

Feeling Lost

Lost in the aisles like a ship at sea,
A map would be handy, oh woe is me!
I wandered by veggies, then straight to snacks,
My shopping list holds no defense against hacks.

An adventure unfolding, it feels quite surreal,
Dairy on my left, frozen meals on the reel.
Is that a pizza? I think it should stay!
But the ice cream is winking, I just can't say nay.

The signs are confusing, do I need pasta?
Or is it sushi, my taste buds got faster?
Chips or crackers, I'm caught in a trance,
Wish I could summon the shopping gods' dance.

Before I know it, my cart starts to overflow,
Just who am I feeding? The world will never know!
With a sigh and a laugh, I finally depart,
A lost little pilgrim, but I'd never outsmart.

The Enlightenment of Grocery Shopping

In the produce section, I ponder my fate,
Shall I hug the kale, or dance with the plate?
Tomatoes are blushing, oh what a plight,
Who knew my grocery run would feel so right?

The cereal aisle calls me, colors so bright,
Frosted flakes? Or just plain old white?
But here comes the milk, with an offer so grand,
A duo of flavors just got out of hand!

Ice cream and pickles, what a curious pair,
But hey, in this moment, I don't even care.
Sour cream dreams and a dash of delight,
I'll wield my cart like a sword in the night.

With each twist and turn, new wonders appear,
The joy of the hunt, oh, it's crystal clear!
A kingdom of goodies, I reign supreme,
Grocery enlightenment, life's silly dream.

The Shopping Cart Chronicles

I roll my cart into a thrilling race,
Dodging old ladies at a rapid pace.
A child is crying, "I want that cake!"
Do I step in or just let them quake?

In the canned goods aisle, it's a fortress of beans,
Each decision feels grand, like I'm saving the scenes.
But what if the peas turn against my will?
Evil green soldiers, oh what a thrill!

The pasta section's a labyrinth of choice,
Fettuccine or penne, I'm losing my voice.
Baffled at flavors, I just stare and stare,
Feeling like I'm the main character of despair.

But as I head out with my cart full of dreams,
I chuckle to myself, life's better than it seems.
Who knew grocery trips could hold so much cheer?
In this bizarre little world, I'm the grocery frontier!

Melons and Metaphysics

A melon's roundness, a cosmic joke,
In the fruit aisle, we ponder folk.
From rinds to seeds, what do they mean?
Are we all just slices in a giant machine?

Bananas hang low, in cheerful descent,
Do they know our time is merely spent?
Or maybe they're plotting to start a band,
With grapes as the audience, oh isn't life grand?

Jars of Forgotten Dreams

On the shelves, jars cluttered with maybes,
Once filled with hopes, now just like babies.
With dusty labels, they sit in a row,
Reminders of wishes where no one can go.

Pickles of passion, salsa of doubt,
What were we thinking—did we just flout?
Each twist of the lid unlocks a scream,
Like unspoken thoughts in the jar of a dream.

The Paradox of the Frozen Aisle

Staring at peas, so frozen in time,
Are they aware they're caught in a rhyme?
The ice cream stares back with a glimmering grin,
Is dessert the answer, or just where we've been?

The meat case whispers of lives gone by,
Yet with each steak, I feel I could fly.
Can we thaw our chances, or leave them as is?
Or shall we just laugh at this frozen quiz?

Navigating the Sea of Labels

In the pasta aisle, I feel quite lost,
Do I want rigatoni or pay the cost?
Each box is a riddle, a puzzling game,
Label to label, it's all quite the same.

Cereal boxes boast of their heights,
While granola delights in its crunchy bites.
But under the flaps, what's hidden inside?
A wilderness of choices, a consumer's pride.

Reflections in the Frozen Aisle

Peering through the chilly glass,
I spy my frozen twin, alas!
She waves with that frosty grin,
As I ponder where I've been.

Each box, a tale of sweet deceit,
The ice cream sings; I'm on my feet.
Is that a pie or a fuzzy friend?
This wondrous cold could never end.

A mountain of peas, a valley of fries,
I question where my sanity lies.
The yogurt giggles, the pizza plots,
In this frozen world, I lose my thoughts.

Yet in the chill, I feel the heat,
Of whimsical wonders and tasty treats.
So here I stand, my cart a throne,
In this frosty realm, I'm all alone!

Celestial Carts and Cosmic Cravings

Galactic carts roll down the lanes,
Filled with chips and cosmic grains.
A soda nebula in my grasp,
With candy comets sure to clasp.

Among the stardust, I ride the wave,
Of cereal boxes, a brave new crave.
To Mars with muffins, to Venus with bread,
Each aisle a cosmos, where dreams are fed.

Jellies orbit like distant stars,
I'm lost in flavors, near and far.
The milk has moons, the bread has rings,
In this universe, my spirit sings.

Returning home, my treasures in tow,
A trip through space, just a bizarre show.
Yet here I am, with laughter and snacks,
In this strange galaxy, no looking back!

The Dance of Labels and Dreams

In the aisle of the mysterious goods,
I tango with labels and misunderstood foods.
A jar of pickles does a jig on the shelf,
While I spin wildly, forgetting myself.

Cereal boxes striking poses so grand,
Each flake whispers secrets, a breakfast band.
The bread rolls out like a padded shoe,
In this dance, I do the cha-cha too.

The pasta sways, the sauces entwined,
Embracing the chaos, I'm humorously blind.
A disco of flavors, the produce is free,
My cart is a partner; it's just you and me.

As I exit this groove, my dance with delight,
I giggle at nectarines shining so bright.
We've waltzed through the whims of the market's tune,
In the dance of the aisles, I feel like a cartoon!

Wandering Between the Offers and Oracles

Beneath the glowing price tags, I roam,
Seeking bargains and a comfortable home.
The oranges hold secrets, the chips hold dreams,
While I bargain-hunt in mad, wild schemes.

Coupons flutter like ethereal wings,
Promises of savings, a chorus that sings.
There's wisdom in yogurt, or so they say,
Navigating sales like a quirky ballet.

I'm lost in this world of flavors and prices,
Where marshmallows boast of their luscious vices.
The checkout line feels like a patient sage,
Whispering tales of an endless page.

Yet in this madness, I find true grace,
Among the products, I've carved my place.
With laughter, I carry my spoils home at last,
In the realm of retail, I'm free and steadfast!

Cartography of Common Goods

In aisle six, a map I find,
With cereal choices, oh so blind.
Each box a treasure, brightly dressed,
Navigating snacks is surely a quest.

To find the cheese that squeaks and glows,
While dodging kids with sticky toes.
Oh look, a tower made of cans,
A snack fort built by tiny hands.

I spy the milk, a sea of white,
Floating atop my cart, a sight!
The yogurt smiles, it's all a joke,
Do they know I'm just a bloke?

In this land of endless rows,
I bargain with my heart, it knows.
Another snack? Or maybe fruit?
Who knew a trip could feel so cute?

Whispers Among Canned Vegetables

In canned corn's silence, secrets hide,
Lentils giggle while peas abide.
Tomatoes squabble in their red suits,
They gossip sweetly 'bout their roots.

In this quiet aisle, I pause to hear,
The chatter of pickles, oh so near.
Carrots tell tales of garden dreams,
While beans plot schemes in their tight seams.

O, cabbage rolls seem wise and sage,
Who knew such drama's on this stage?
Potatoes ponder their earthly fate,
As I just stand here—should I wait?

An audience lost in the veggie lore,
This supermarket becomes so much more.
With every aisle, a new debut,
In this comedy, I'm thoroughly skewed.

The Kaleidoscope of Flavors

A swirl of colors, bright and bold,
Fruit's laughter and spices unfold.
The orange of zest, the green of thyme,
Each jar of jam sings its own rhyme.

The honey's sticky, golden glow,
As strawberries plot an ambush below.
A citrus chorus fills the air,
I tap my feet, without a care.

Herbs in a dance, so lively and spry,
Mixing and mingling, oh my, oh my!
In pesto dreams and salsa blurs,
Flavors frolic like dancing spurs.

This kaleidoscope spins, it bends and weaves,
Where every taste is more than it leaves.
I grab a basket, what a delight,
To cook and feast through day and night!

Aisle 9: Where Time Stands Still

Aisle Nine, oh, what a sight,
Shampoos giggling in morning light.
While soap whispers tales of cleanliness,
I stand entranced in this silliness.

With each step, I lose the clock,
Detergent dances, oh what a shock!
Toothpaste rows, a minty cheer,
How long have I been standing here?

The razors wink with gleaming pride,
Inviting me for a closer ride.
Deodorants whisper secrets sweet,
In this aisle, life's a graceful feat.

Time ticks by, but here I stay,
In a beauty ballet, quite the display.
Each product shines, each label glows,
A comedy show that never slows!

Beyond the Cart: Transitory Thoughts

In the aisle of dreams, I wander,
What's that smell? Is it me or the plunder?
Items dance, with price tags in tow,
Do I really need twenty cans of faux?

The cereal's a riddle, a colorful maze,
Frosted or crunchy? It's a cereal craze!
Do I want to be happy or just feel full?
Waiting for answers, I'm losing my cool.

Lost in the maze, with a cart as my guide,
Who thought a lettuce could make me decide?
Life choices mixed with the brands that I know,
Ketchup or mustard? Just let it all flow!

Before checkout, I panic and freeze,
Do I really want this much cheese?
A chuckle escapes as I now understand,
The treasures of life come in bags from the land!

The Still Life of Shopping

A tomato lies quiet, deep red and round,
Am I just a shopper or lost and unbound?
Strawberries beckon, they've made quite the fuss,
What flavors distract me from this shopping bus?

The salads are glancing with dressing options wide,
Should I go creamy or more on the side?
To choose between greens becomes quite the art,
Yet here I am lost, with a half-hearted cart.

Around me, cereal boxes hold secrets untold,
Who knew they'd provoke such thoughts bold?
A bite of the pastel promises laughter and fun,
Or at least blurry visions of lost snacks on the run!

As I reach for the milk, it slips from my grip,
Who knew that dairy could lead to this trip?
It splatters my path, is it chaos or fate?
Life's greatest moments can come from a crate!

Reflections Among the Sodas

Bubbles in cans, they giggle and pop,
Should I take cola, or just soda shop?
A fizzy decision, a bubbly delight,
But which one grants me a caffeine-filled night?

Candy aisles sparkle like jewels in the sun,
Oh, the crunchy treasures! This could be fun.
Gumdrops and lollies, a sweet summer treat,
But will I regret it—a sugary feat?

As I ponder my choices and sway left and right,
A jester appears, quite the comedic sight!
Is he part of my quest for the ultimate snack,
Or just here to lighten this shopping attack?

With bags in tow, I navigate my way,
Life's little puzzles unfold in this play.
The checkout is nearing, my cart's now divine,
In the land of the market, I'm feeling just fine!

The Meandering Mind in Aisle Twelve

In aisle twelve, my thoughts start to wander,
What's that smell? Is it freshness I ponder?
Or is it the broccoli, lurking nearby,
With whispers of health that make me comply?

The soaps and the cleansers, they glisten and shine,
Scented like roses, this could be divine!
Yet as I consider, what scent to embrace,
My mind drifts to cupcakes — a sweet little place.

I grab chips and salsa, the perfect pair,
But wait, why envision a party to share?
This cart's becoming a world of its own,
With snacks and delights, I feel less alone!

Finally I chuckle, near registers' glare,
This is my adventure, no need for despair!
The supermarket's magic, its odd little spell,
Turns everyday shopping to tales I can tell!

The Last Cereal Box

In the aisle of breakfast dreams,
A box stands tall, or so it seems.
I reach for it, my heart skips a beat,
Will it be crispy or soggy wheat?

A prize inside, oh what a tease,
A toy or trinket, oh please, oh please!
I grasp it tight like a winning ticket,
But then it slips — oh, is it wicked?

The shelf is bare, I'm left to pout,
Did I need it? Hmm, without a doubt!
A playful jog down this endless lane,
What's life without a little grain?

As I clear the aisle with half a frown,
I realize I'm just a cereal clown.
At checkout now, I look so meek,
But in my heart, I've found my peak!

Labyrinth of Choices

A cart with wheels that twist and turn,
In rows of snacks, my head will churn.
Should I grab chips or maybe sweets?
Oh, what a puzzle, my heart repeats!

Pickles or olives, oh what to choose?
In this maze, I cannot lose.
I ask a stranger for advice,
She shrugs — guess it's not that nice!

A flashing sale sign catches my eye,
Is the deal too good? I cannot lie!
A box of crackers caught in suspense,
Thoughts of clearance make no sense!

But hey, ten for four? Let's have a ball,
My cart now fills — what's good? What's small?
With laughter in this aisle of fate,
I leave with snacks, and that feels great!

Reflections in the Checkout Mirror

In the shiny glass, I see my fate,
A visage crammed with snacks innate.
The line is slow, a tortoise race,
But what's the rush in this funny place?

I check the items, they wink and nudge,
Do I really need this embarrassing fudge?
A quick glance at my guilty stash,
Oh, to name it all would be quite brash!

The lady in front, her cart's a tale,
Toilet paper, snacks, a curious trail.
She flashes me a smile, so wide!
In this odd spectacle, we take pride.

Lastly, my turn at the screen so bright,
I toss the items, oh what a sight!
But I leave with glee, no doubt or fear,
For laughter's the key — let's bring some cheer!

When Loyalty Cards Become Life Lessons

Swipe the card, what do I gain?
A point here and there, am I going insane?
With tiny rewards that stack like hay,
Do I build a barn or throw them away?

The checkout clerk, she laughs and grins,
Says, "Keep collecting — you'll win big wins!"
But what's the prize, a coupon or two?
In this buffet of life, what's really true?

As I juggle my memories of sales and deals,
I ponder the meaning that fortune reveals.
Is loyalty just love in disguise?
Or a game of chance masked by coupons and lies?

With pockets bulging and thoughts a whirl,
I realize, it's just a crazy world.
But here I stand, and laugh a bit,
In this grocery life, I truly fit!

The Ephemeral Nature of Freshness

In the aisle of greens, they dance and sway,
Forgotten herbs whisper secrets of decay.
Tomatoes blush, but their days are few,
Salad dreams are lost, in a drizzle of dew.

Mold reigns supreme over bread like a crown,
While yogurt rebels, refusing to frown.
Bananas spot their future, ripe with dread,
They laugh at the fate of the soon-to-be bread.

Pickles in jars, a briny ballet,
Awkwardly lurking, just a cart ride away.
Cheese, ever smelly, throws parties at midnight,
When the fridge door creaks, it stirs up a fight.

Among the wrappers, secrets abound,
Life's fleeting freshness, an odd little sound.
Yet in this chaos, giggles persist,
In the mad, merry mess that we all can't resist.

Juxtaposition of Carts and Contemplation

Two carts collide in a cosmic spree,
One's full of dreams, the other, brie.
Beneath fluorescent lights, deep thoughts ignite,
Like cereal boxes debating their plight.

The cookie aisle calls with a siren's song,
While kale stands stoic, whispering, 'You're wrong.'
Do I pick dessert or a fiber-rich boon?
The answer might come with the next full moon.

In a sea of brands, I lose my way,
A snack-sized dilemma holds sway today.
Chips grin slyly, and nuts throw a ruckus,
Where's the logic in this grocery circus?

Philosophers ponder, we shoppers just grin,
As the self-checkout laughs at the chaos within.
In this carted confusion, we find our delight,
Each choice a jest, in artificial light.

Unwrapping the Layers of Reality

Tinfoil wrapped dreams, layers to unfold,
Zucchini's a gnome with treasures untold.
Peeling back onions, we cry and we cheer,
Each layer reveals something oddly sincere.

A banana with freckles, a fruit gone to show,
Reflects on its fading, a yellowed tableau.
The celery sticks stand, all green and austere,
While grapes roll their eyes, gossiping near.

Silly bagged lettuce with its crunch and its crunch,
Mocks radishes masked like a punch-drunk munch.
The wraps and the boxes, a loud paper tease,
In the clutches of shopping, our worries can freeze.

So unwrap the reality, slice it with cheer,
In the deli of dreams, have another cold beer!
For every small moment we share with a snack,
Is a ribbon of joy that we never look back.

The Mystery of Missing Shopping Lists

I started my quest with a list tied to fate,
Yet somehow it vanished, just like my weight.
Apples and oranges danced in my head,
But the salsa I craved? Just slumbered instead.

A script of my cravings, gone with the breeze,
Forgotten like socks in the laundry, with ease.
Do I bribe the ice cream or plead to the bread?
Each aisle becomes riddled - which way lies my head?

The popcorn is beckoning, 'Choose me, take flight!'
But does it pair well with my hot dog delight?
A quest for existence held captive by snacks,
Will I discover the truth, or just end up with flax?

In this labyrinth of choices, I wander, I roam,
My heart's a mere shopper, out searching for home.
But hidden within, like a prank from the shelf,
Are the memories made when we're lost in ourselves.

Aisle by Aisle

In the cereal row, I ponder my fate,
Crunchy or flakey, oh what a debate!
Cart in a whirl, I spin like a top,
Lost in the colors where breakfast won't stop.

Soup cans whisper tales of the past,
Each label a hint, a shadow that's cast.
I search for the meaning behind every broth,
Is this carrot real, or just a mirthful cloth?

Dairy delights, a creamy affair,
I flirt with the cheese, ignoring the glare.
Yogurt in pots, like tiny little worlds,
I scoop up the essence, as laughter unfurls.

Check-out line queues, a surreal parade,
Who knew that coupons could become a charade?
As I rattle my change, I ponder my buy,
Did I need that last item? Oh, well, I'll try!

A Journey of Intent

With a cart like a ship, I sail down the lane,
Navigating treasures in ketchup and grain.
Pickles and onions, they dance in my mind,
Is it dinner or chaos? I can't seem to find.

Oh shelf of spices, a rainbow of flair,
What do I need? A pinch or a scare?
Paprika sings praise, while cumin looks shy,
In this whimsical kingdom, I'm the reigning guy.

Frozen delights, penguins ice-skate,
I hover and ponder, it's never too late!
Pizza or broccoli? What's under the frost?
My hunger's a shipwreck, and I'm feeling lost.

As I trek to the sweets, my heart takes a leap,
In the land of the candy, temptation runs deep.
The chocolate bars whisper, "Just one little bite!"
What's one more indulgence in this delectable night?

Reality Bottled and Boxed

In the aisles of glass, dreams bottled tight,
Juice drinks in hues that dance in the light.
Each label, a promise, a send-off to cheer,
But really, what's juice? Is it friendship or beer?

Boxes stacked high, like a tower of fate,
Is this dinner for one, or a banquet I hate?
Mac and cheese winks, "I'll fill you with glee,"
While sushi rolls beckon, "Come play cook with me!"

The bakery beckons with a sweet siren's call,
Croissants and bagels, they're having a ball.
I jostle my cart, growing heavy with treats,
A laugh from the donut, sweet hole in its beats.

At the end of each aisle, fate always lurks,
A sandwich that whispers, "You've gone to the works!"
But who's keeping score on this quest for the best?
In the land of the market, I'm simply a guest!

Surreal Shadows in the Snack Alley

In the shadows of snacks, a circus unfolds,
Potato chips giggle as their story's retold.
Popcorn like clouds with a buttery gleam,
Can movie night dreams turn into a meme?

Chocolates in wrappers, each face tells a tale,
Some strut with pride, while others go pale.
With jellybeans jiving, I just can't resist,
What flavor am I? Oh, I'm lost in the mist!

Taco-flavored nachos, what a curious sound,
A fiesta of flavors, I'm upside down!
As pretzels pirouette, so crunchy, so grand,
Who knew that a snack could lead to this band?

In the end cap's grace, I linger and peek,
Soda cans chatter, they're quenching their streak.
Each sip is a giggle, a tickle, a tease,
In the land of the snacks, I'm forever at ease!

Navigating the Maze of Choices

Lost in a maze where decisions collide,
Each aisle a passage, my thoughts like a tide.
Should I pick garlic or settle for spice?
The choices are plenty, it's rolling the dice!

Frozen treats whisper, "We're here for the fun!"
Ice cream and sorbet? Can't pick just one.
Taste buds are laughing as flavors parade,
I'm lost in a carnival, sweet dreams are made.

Green veggies stand tall, all prim and so neat,
While candy bars call me, "Come join the sweet heat!"
Shakes rattle my brain as I navigate round,
In this joyous riddle, what's lost can be found.

At checkout, I sigh, it's time to go home,
With treasures collected, together we roam.
What was it I wanted? Oh, what did it mean?
In the market of life, I'm the jester, the queen!

The Poet's Pantry

In aisles where dreams collide with bread,
I found a shelf of words unsaid,
Muffins whisper secrets in a row,
Spices grin, 'Add us to your show!'

Cart wheels squeak like a pen on paper,
Bananas giggle—nature's caper,
While pickles plot a zesty scheme,
And chips crinkle, 'Join our team!'

Sometimes I muse on fruits and yogurt,
What lives in these jars where laughs are courted?
Ketchup calls, "Don't take me too serious!"
As I stroll through aisles, my mind is curious!

With each coupon clipped, my soul runs free,
In this quirky land, I just might be,
The poet of produce, the bard of beans,
Crafting verses 'mongst grocery means!

Riddles Among the Cereal Boxes

A tower of boxes, brightly dressed,
Tell tales with crunch, they jest and jest.
Captain Crunch wears a silly hat,
While Frosted Flakes make my heart go splat!

Oats laugh softly, a wholesome cheer,
As Cocoa Puffs shout, "We're the best here!"
I tiptoe past, with a grin so wide,
Together we ponder—the milk or the ride?

Honeycombs buzz with buzz without ends,
Cheerios sigh, 'We just want some friends!'
Under a moonlit, fluorescent gleam,
I search for reality in the sugary dream.

Cornflakes stand stoically, all square,
While Rice Krispies snap at their airy air,
In this riddle of breakfast encased in a box,
Laughter echoes, like playful clocks.

Counting on Boxes to Fill the Void

Stacks of pasta whisper from the shelf,
I ponder deeply: 'Who am I, myself?'
A world of boxes, tall and round,
Each a potential friend to be found.

Canned beans await with stories untold,
"Join us!" they beckon, "We're spicy and bold!"
I ponder hard, how to fill my cart,
With laughter as the currency, dear to my heart.

Popcorn's popping as if to cheer,
While sweets plot schemes to bring me near,
Almonds crack jokes from their crunchy space,
In this market of joy, I find my place.

Yet here I stand, confused and spry,
Collecting boxes as moments fly by,
The void can't be filled by just any food,
But laughter, my friend, can change my mood!

Grocery Store Grapevine: Secrets and Solitude

In the corner, a potato leans and sighs,
"I know secrets—but who am I to advise?"
Carrots giggle, dressed in green,
While broccoli broods, feeling unseen.

The lettuce whispers of scandals past,
Every crunchy leaf seems to have a blast,
With each swipe down the toothpaste lane,
I hear gossip spreading—oh, such disdain!

Eggplants huddle, exchanging their tales,
While tomato sauce screams out, "No more fails!"
A banana slips on the gossip train,
In solitude of peas, we all entertain.

Lost among products, I contemplate fate,
This grapevine of chatter isn't so great,
Yet through the folly of produce and calls,
In this supermarket, every secret enthralls!

www.ingramcontent.com/pod-product-compliance
Ingram Content Group UK Ltd.
Pitfield, Milton Keynes, MK11 3LW, UK
UKHW021648160125
4146UKWH00033B/647